HISTORY UNCUT

THE REAL
Benedict Arnold

Virginia Loh-Hagan

45th Parallel Press

Published in the United States of America by Cherry Lake Publishing
Ann Arbor, Michigan
www.cherrylakepublishing.com

Reading Adviser: Marla Conn MS, Ed., Literacy specialist, Read-Ability, Inc.
Book Designer: Felicia Macheske

Photo Credits: © Amy Nichole Harris/Shutterstock.com, cover, 1; © Everett Historical/Shutterstock.com, 5, 30;
© ChameleonsEye/Shutterstock.com, 7; © Underwood & Underwood. A Ball-Room Scene in Colonial Days—Our
Great-Grand-Parents Were Young Once Too. United States, ca. 1900. New York, N.Y.: Underwood & Underwood,
Jul. 25. Photograph. Retrieved from the Library of Congress, https://www.loc.gov/item/2006676723/;
© Mark Grenier/Shutterstock.com, 11; © Jim Hawthorn/Shutterstock.com, 12; © Everett Historical/Shutterstock.
com, 15; © borsmenta/Shutterstock.com, 17; © Joseph Sohm/Shutterstock.com, 19; © Labrador Photo Video/
Shutterstock.com, 20; © FotoDuets/Shutterstock.com, 23; © Katsiuba Volha/Shutterstock.com, 24; © Chromakey/
Shutterstock.com, 27; © Africa Studio/Shutterstock.com, 29

Graphic Elements Throughout: © iulias/Shutterstock.com; © Thinglass/Shutterstock.com; © kzww/Shutterstock.
com; © A_Lesik/Shutterstock.com; © MegaShabanov/Shutterstock.com; © Groundback Atelier/Shutterstock.com;
© saki80/Shutterstock.com

45th Parallel Press is an imprint of Cherry Lake Publishing.

Library of Congress Cataloging-in-Publication Data has been filed and is available at catalog.loc.gov

Cherry Lake Publishing would like to acknowledge the work of The Partnership for 21st Century Skills.
Please visit www.p21.org for more information.

Printed in the United States of America
Corporate Graphics

Table of Contents

CHAPTER 1

Benedict Arnold
The Story You Know

Benedict Arnold was a soldier. He fought in the American Revolution. Revolution is an overthrow. The United States was owned by Great Britain. It wanted to be its own country. It wanted independence. Independence means freedom. This war took place from 1775 to 1783.

Arnold fought in the American army. He fought against the British army. He was a war hero. But he's famous for being a traitor. Traitors are people who betray. Arnold was a spy. He gave away information. He switched sides. He became a British soldier. He was a hated man. But there's more to his story…

At this time, the United States was known as the American colonies.

CHAPTER 2

Patriotic Roots

Arnold was born on January 14, 1741. He was born in Connecticut. His family was very **patriotic**. Patriotic means being devoted to one's country. Many of his family members served the country. The Arnolds were a political family. They were a military family. They're important to U.S. history.

Arnold was named after his great-grandfather. His great-grandfather was the first governor of Rhode Island. Arnold was also related to John Lothropp. Lothropp was one of the early settlers in New England. He supported the separation of church and state. His family line produced 6 U.S. presidents.

Arnold is related to George W. Bush.

SETTING THE WORLD STAGE
1741

▸ The New York Slave Rebellion took place in 1741. White, rich New Yorkers thought black slaves and poor whites were making plans. They thought there was a plan to set fire to the city. Over 150 people were arrested. About 30 blacks and 4 whites were exiled. Exiled means kicked out.

▸ Vitus Bering was a Danish explorer. He worked for Russia. He was an officer in the Russian navy. He discovered Alaska in 1741. He saw a sea between Asia and America. He got lost in a storm. He ended up in Alaska. Many places are named after him.

▸ Maria Theresa ruled Austria. She ruled for over 40 years. She was the only female ruler of the Hapsburg lands. She was crowned Queen of Hungary in 1741. She gave birth to 16 children. Her most famous child was Marie Antoinette.

"What do you think would be my fate if my misguided countrymen were to take me prisoner?" –Benedict Arnold

Arnold's mother was part of the Lothropp family line. She was rich. She and Arnold's father had 6 children. Only Arnold and a sister lived. His other **siblings** died from **yellow fever**. Siblings are brothers and sisters. Yellow fever is a sickness. It's spread by mosquitoes. It can be deadly.

Arnold's father was sad. He drank a lot. He lost the family money. Arnold's mother died. So, Arnold stepped up. He took care of his father and sister.

Arnold married Margaret Mansfield. Mansfield was the sheriff's daughter. They had 3 children. Mansfield died. Arnold married again. He married Peggy Shippen. Shippen was from a rich family. The Shippens were judges and lawyers. Arnold and Shippen had 5 children.

Arnold was involved with many rich and important families.

CHAPTER 3

War Hero

Arnold was a great war general. He took part in many military missions. He was brave. He was smart. His actions helped win the Revolution.

Arnold built one of the first American navy **fleets**. Fleets are groups of ships. A British fleet was planning an attack. Arnold had ships built. He fought back. He slowed down the British attack. He forced them to change their plans.

He led Connecticut troops. He took gunpowder. He helped capture Fort Ticonderoga. He took their supplies.

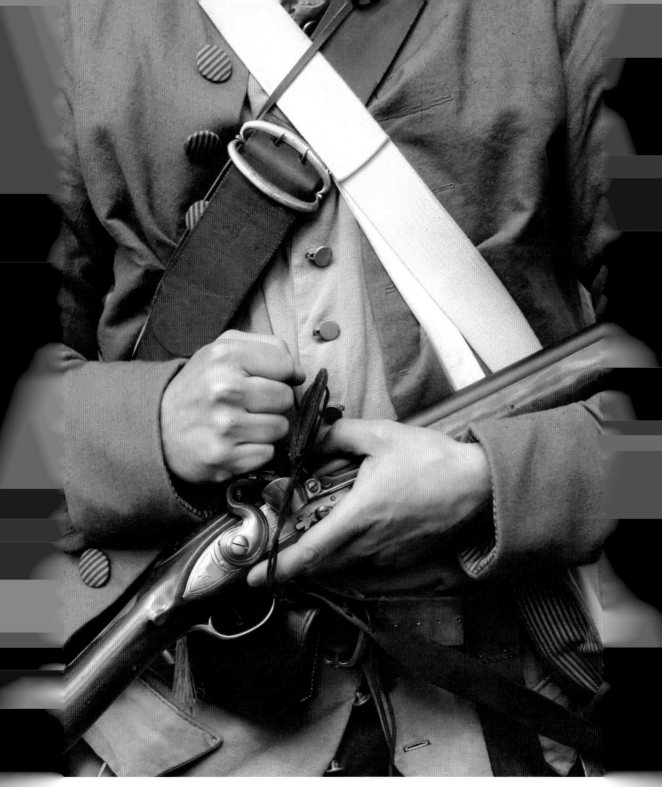

Arnold used his own money to train his soldiers.

The British were attacking from Canada. Arnold marched with over 1,000 men. He wanted to capture Quebec to stop them.

He helped win the Battle of Saratoga. This battle was a turning point. The French decided to help the United States. Their help won the war. But during the battle, Arnold got shot. A bullet went through his leg. It killed his horse. The horse fell on Arnold. It crushed his left leg.

Arnold walked with a limp. One leg was 2 inches (5 centimeters) shorter than the other. But he became a war hero. People thought he was brave. They thought he was a good leader.

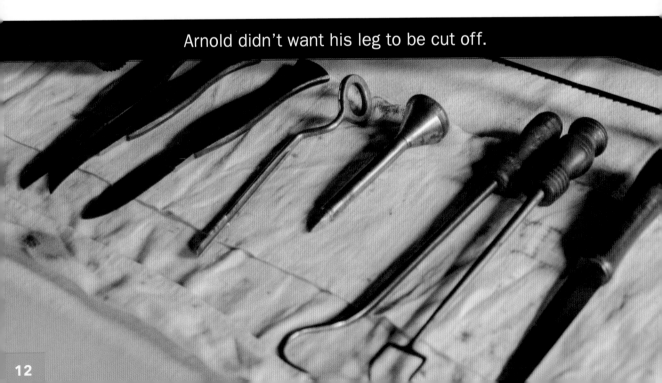
Arnold didn't want his leg to be cut off.

All in the Family

Henry Arnold was born in 1886. He's related to Benedict Arnold. He was a great soldier. He graduated from West Point. He was in the U.S. Army Air Forces. He was a general in World War II. He led air battles. He helped win the war. He was chief of the Army Air Corps. He earned a five-star rank as general of the Air Force. He was the first to do so. He helped develop military aviation. Aviation is flying. The Wright brothers taught him how to fly. Henry Arnold was one of the first military pilots. He used radio to report what he saw. He was the first to do this. He supported making new planes. He supported building flight schools. He trained pilots. He wrote books. He worked as a stunt pilot for silent movies. He was called "Hap." This was short for "happy." He died in 1950.

"Love to my country actuates my present conduct. However, it may appear inconsistent to the world, who very seldom judge right of any man's actions." –Benedict Arnold

CHAPTER 4

Switching Sides

Arnold had friends. But he also had enemies. People didn't like him. They worked against him. They took credit for his work. This made Arnold mad.

Arnold didn't get promoted. He kept getting passed up. The American government promoted 5 junior officers. They didn't promote him. This offended Arnold.

Shippen's family may have been **Loyalists**. Loyalists supported the British. Arnold and Shippen lived a rich life. They spent a lot of money. They ran out of money. They owed money. This made people doubt Arnold. They accused him of abusing his powers. They thought he used his power to get money.

There are many reasons why Arnold became
a traitor. Mainly, he felt disrespected.

THAT
Happened?!?

Many people get hurt in war. Some people lose their legs. Hannah Campbell is a British soldier. She fought in Iraq. A bomb went off. It buried Campbell alive. It crushed her leg. It split her hand. A metal pole stabbed her face. It blinded one of her eyes. Another pole stabbed her lung. Her brain was bleeding. She had 18 operations. She lost one of her legs. Rick Clement is a British soldier. He fought in Afghanistan. He was hit with a bomb. He lost both legs. His hip broke in two. His stomach was damaged. His right arm was damaged. Campbell and Clement were at the same hospital. They fell in love. They understood each other. Campbell said, "I fancy Rick. I find him attractive on many levels. But I also believe he's my soul mate."

Arnold was investigated. He was cleared of charges. But he was mad. He said, "Having made every **sacrifice** of fortune and blood, and become a cripple in the service of my country, I little expected to meet the ungrateful returns I have received from my countrymen." Sacrifice means giving something up.

Arnold also lost faith. Soldiers were treated badly. People were hungry. Arnold thought the country was doing worse. He thought British rule might be better. He didn't think the United States could win.

So, he switched sides. He used his wife's connections. He contacted British officials. He said he was willing to betray the United States. But he wanted to get paid.

Shippen hosted many parties. Loyalists were there.

CHAPTER 5

A Traitor is Born

Arnold passed secret messages to the British. He wrote in code. He used **invisible** ink. Invisible means it can't be seen. Arnold sent reports. He gave information about the American troops. He shared where they were going. He shared where supplies were. Shippen helped. She delivered messages.

Arnold secretly met with John André. André was a British officer. Arnold and André **plotted**. Plot is to make a secret plan. Arnold was to **surrender** West Point. Surrender means to give up. West Point was a military fort. It was an important defense.

West Point is a military school today.

Arnold got command of West Point. He planned on giving it to the British. He was going to get a lot of money. So, he started to weaken the fort. He didn't repair anything. He drained supplies.

But American forces captured André. André had papers. He hid papers in his boot. The papers described the plot. André was charged as a spy. He was hanged.

Arnold heard about André's capture. He ran away. He fled to a British ship. He escaped American troops.

Americans hated Arnold. But his **treason** brought them together. Treason means betrayal. Arnold brought energy back to the Americans' cause.

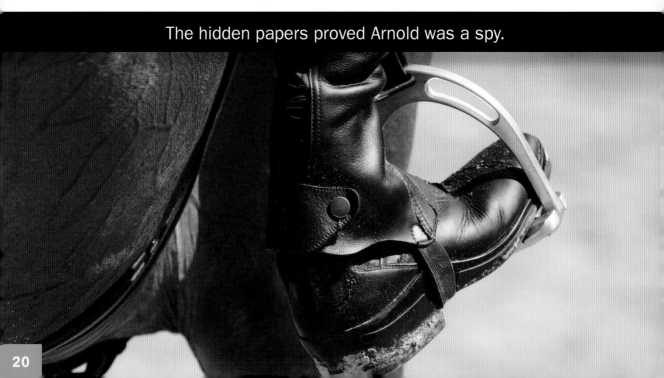
The hidden papers proved Arnold was a spy.

Bad Blood

Arnold had a bad temper. He got mad quickly. He fought in duels. Duels are fights between 2 people. Croskie was a British sea captain. He invited Arnold to a party. Arnold forgot to go. He said sorry. But Croskie was mad. He called Arnold a name. He said Arnold had bad manners. Arnold didn't like that. He wanted to protect his honor. He demanded a duel. Arnold and Croskie agreed to fight. They used guns. Croskie took the first shot. He missed. Then, Arnold shot. He shot him in the arm. He wanted to shoot again. He said, "I give you notice. If you miss this time, I shall kill you." But Croskie said no. The fight was over. This duel took place in Honduras.

"None but Almighty God shall prevent my marching!"
— Benedict Arnold

CHAPTER 6

Beyond the Betrayal

Arnold gave reasons for his actions. He wrote a letter. The letter was published in newspapers. Its title was "To the **Inhabitants** of America." Inhabitants means people who live in a place. Arnold blamed the American government. He accused them of poor leadership. He asked Americans to return to British rule. This made some Americans even madder. They called him evil.

Arnold was made a British general. He took charge of Loyalist troops in New York. He led raids in Virginia. He led raids in Connecticut. He sacked cities. He burned buildings. He burned ships. He took supplies.

Arnold didn't agree with the United States' partnership with France.

John Champe was sent to kidnap Arnold. He became a spy. He joined Arnold's team. He planned to take Arnold during his night walk. But plans changed. Arnold was sent away. The plot was ruined.

Americans won the war. They hated Arnold. Arnold moved his family to London. But he wasn't liked there, either. British people blamed him for André's death. They wrote bad things about him. They blocked him from getting jobs.

Arnold moved to Canada. He started a business. But Canadians hated him, too. So, he moved back to London.

◀ Canadians burned a statue of Arnold.

CHAPTER 7

Not Your Average Spy

Arnold is known as a traitor. But he was more than that. In his early life, he was a successful businessman. When his father died, he made money. He worked with his mother's family. The Lothropps taught him about business. Arnold became a **pharmacist**. Pharmacists sold medicine. He did other things. He sold books. He became a trader. He bought 3 ships. He traveled. He made lots of money. He paid off debts. He took care of his family. The British taxed his businesses. He thought this was unfair. He fought back. This is why he joined the American Revolution. But his good deeds have been forgotten.

Pharmacists make and sell medicines.

Explained by
SCIENCE

Everybody lies. People tell big lies. They tell little lies. There are different types of lying. People make up stories. They cover things up. Traitors and spies lie a lot. They lie all the time. They pretend to be different people. It's easy to lie with words. But it's not easy to lie with body actions. People lose eye focus. They can't control their hands. They stand in different ways. They sweat. They get nervous. Their heart rate increases. When lying, body language doesn't match words. Liars spend more time on words. They lose track of their body. To detect lying, pay attention to the body. People get better at lying. One lie leads to more lies. Brain scientists looked at people's brains. Reactions for lies decreases each time. This means lying gets easier over time.

"Let me die in this old uniform in which I fought my battles. May God forgive me for ever having put on another." — Benedict Arnold

Arnold died on June 14, 1801. He died in London. He died in pain. He died a hated man. He didn't have any military honors.

He's buried in London. He's buried at St. Mary's Church. He's buried in the basement. There's a sign marking his tomb. It reads, "The two nations whom he served in turn in the years of their **enmity** have united in enduring friendship." Enmity means bad feelings.

Bill Stanley is a former state senator. He's from Arnold's hometown. He paid for the sign. He said, "He saved America before he betrayed it."

Arnold could only walk with a cane.

Timeline

1741 Arnold was born. He was the fifth person in his family to be named Benedict Arnold.

1755 Arnold heard a military drummer. He wanted to join the military. His mother wouldn't let him.

1757 Arnold joined the local Connecticut military. He fought in the French and Indian War.

1761 Arnold's father died. He had been a drunk. Arnold tried to restore the family name.

1767 Arnold married Margaret Mansfield. Mansfield was around 17 years old.

1775 Arnold seized control of New York's Fort Ticonderoga. Ticonderoga was a British fort. It was easily won. It inspired Arnold's interest in military strategy.

1775 Arnold invaded Canada. His men marched 350 miles (563 kilometers) through rain, snow, and ice. They ate candles, dogs, and shoe leather. He got shot in the leg.

1777 Arnold helped win the Battle of Saratoga. The British wanted to control New York. They wanted to separate northern and southern colonies. They thought this would end the war. Arnold hurt his leg a second time.

1778 Arnold went to Valley Forge. He participated in the first recorded Oath of Allegiance. He vowed to be loyal to the United States.

1778 Arnold became commander of Philadelphia. His hurt leg meant he couldn't fight anymore.

1779 Arnold married Peggy Shippen. Some of Shippen's family members had been in the Philadelphia government.

1779 Arnold was sent to court twice. He was accused of misusing government resources. He was accused of illegal trading.

1779 Arnold began writing to John André.

1780 Arnold became commander of West Point.

1781 Arnold moved to London.

1801 Arnold died. He was 60 years old.

Consider This!

Take a Position! Arnold was a war hero. And he was a traitor. Which one do you think he was more of? Argue your point with reasons and evidence.

Say What? Learn more about the American Revolution. Explain Arnold's role in the war. How did he help?

Think About It! George Washington said, "Arnold has betrayed us! Whom can we trust now?" People sometimes call each other "Benedict Arnold." This means someone is a traitor. Has anyone betrayed you? What happened?

Learn More

Burgan, Michael, and Terry Beatty (illust.). *Benedict Arnold: American Hero and Traitor*. Mankato, MN: Capstone Press, 2007.

Castrovilla, Selene, and John O'Brien (illust.). *Revolutionary Rogues: Benedict Arnold and John André*. Honesdale, PA: Calkins Creek, 2017.

Gunderson, Jessica. *Benedict Arnold: Battlefield Hero or Selfish Traitor?* North Mankato, MN: Capstone Press, 2014.

Glossary

enmity (EN-mih-tee) bad feelings; ill will

fleets (FLEETS) groups of ships or planes traveling together

independence (in-dih-PEN-duhns) freedom

inhabitants (in-HAB-ih-tuhnts) people living in a certain place

invisible (in-VIZ-uh-buhl) not able to be seen

Loyalists (LOI-uhl-ists) people who were loyal to the British and supported the American colonies staying under British rule

patriotic (pay-tree-AH-tik) being devoted to one's country

pharmacist (FAHR-muh-sist) a person who sells medicine

plotted (PLAHT-ed) planned in secret

revolution (rev-uh-LOO-shuhn) an overthrow; getting rid of an old system for a new system

sacrifice (SAK-ruh-fise) the act of giving up something for something else

siblings (SIB-lingz) brothers or sisters

surrender (suh-REN-dur) to give up

traitor (TRAY-tur) a person who betrays

treason (TREE-zuhn) the act of betraying

yellow fever (YEL-oh FEE-vur) a disease that is spread by infected mosquitoes

Index

About the Author

Dr. Virginia Loh-Hagan is an author, university professor, former classroom teacher, and curriculum designer. She was born on June 14. Benedict Arnold died on June 14. She lives in San Diego with her very tall husband and very naughty dogs. To learn more about her, visit www.virginialoh.com.